Mammals and Their Milk

Lucia Anderson · Illustrated by Jennifer Dewey

Dodd, Mead & Company · New York

To Greta — L.A.
To Tamar — J.D.

Distributed in Canada by McClelland and Stewart Limited, Toronto
Printed in Hong Kong by South China Printing Company
1 2 3 4 5 6 7 8 9 10

Library of Congress Cataloging in Publication Data
Anderson, Lucia.
   Mammals and their milk.
   Summary: Discusses that aspect of mammalian physiology
which produces milk and feed it to mammal babies.
   1. Mammals — Physiology — Juvenile literature.
2. Mammary glands — Juvenile literature.   3. Milk —
Juvenile literature   4. Lactation — Juvenile literature.
[1. Mammals — Physiology.   2. Mammary glands.   3. Milk.
4. Lactation] I. Dewey, Jennifer, ill. II. Title.
QL739.2.A53   1984   599′.016   84-13522
ISBN 0-396-08317-X

In our world, all living things are able to reproduce, to make more of their own kind that will take their places when they die. By reproducing, one generation of plants or animals gives rise to another, and life does not stop. That is part of the reason life has lasted on this planet several billion years.

Young plants and animals do not always have an easy time, however. They may have trouble finding food, or they may get sick, or their enemies may eat them. So, in the long span of time that living things have inhabited our planet, they have evolved different ways of reproducing to improve their chances of survival from one generation to the next.

The simplest forms of life reproduce just by splitting in half over and over.

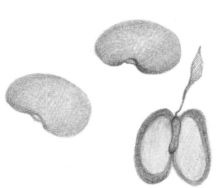

More complex forms reproduce when a sperm cell from the male joins, or fertilizes, an egg cell from the female. The union starts to divide. Two, four, eight cells, then sixteen, thirty-two...a tiny piece of life has begun. This speck of life is called an embryo. It is the baby plant or animal starting to form, and it is very fragile. Embryos of flowering plants grow inside seeds, surrounded by food and protected by sturdy coverings.

Animal embryos are fed and protected in different ways.

Some grow inside of fertilized eggs. Eggs are neat bundles assembled inside a mother's body. They contain everything the embryos need—a surrounding sac of food and a protective shell or coating. Some animals lay hundreds of eggs at once, so there are many chances for at least a few to survive and establish the next generation.

After the eggs are laid, the embryos inside grow bigger and stronger on the food around them. When the food is used up, the baby animals hatch. Unless they are birds, their mothers are probably nowhere around. Now how will they get their food?

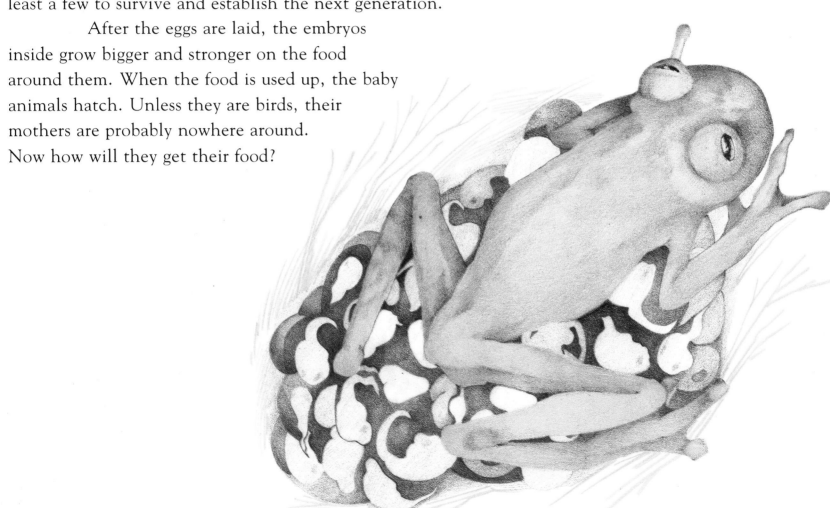

Tadpoles catch little creatures in the ponds where they have hatched. But sometimes larger pond animals eat them before they can grow into frogs.

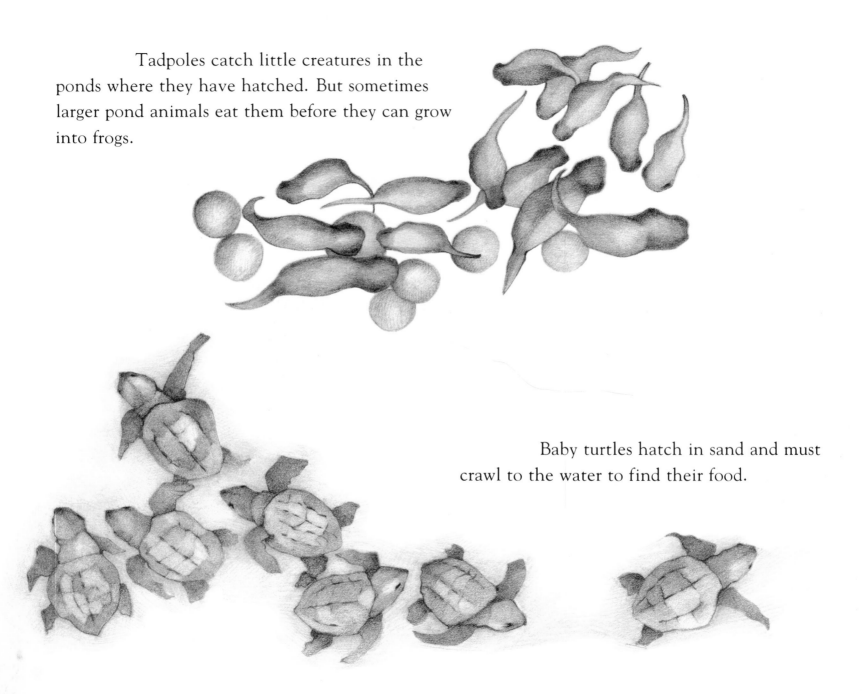

Baby turtles hatch in sand and must crawl to the water to find their food.

Spider mothers often lay their eggs on insects they have killed. When the young hatch, their food is waiting for them.

Baby fish swim off to find food. Sometimes they are eaten by bigger fish before they have a chance to grow.

Most baby birds stay in their nests and eat food their parents bring them. Birds lay only a few eggs at a time and take more care of their young than do animals that leave lots of eggs behind.

But there are many animals that do not lay eggs. Embryos of these animals grow inside their mothers' bodies for quite a while, using their mothers' food and energy. Usually only one or a few embryos grow at the same time, never hundreds. When these babies are born, they are not encased in protective shells. They enter this world alive, small, and usually helpless. Their mothers take care of them so that they will survive and help establish the next generation.

Where do these babies get their food? They do not have to go out and find it. And their mothers do not have to go out and find it for them, either. These babies get a perfect food right from their mothers' bodies. Their mothers make it just for them. The food is milk.

Animals that begin life by drinking their mother's milk are called *mammals*. You are a mammal—your first food was milk. Your mother's milk helped you grow strong and healthy. Or you may have been fed milk made by another mammal, a cow, or perhaps even a goat.

The special places on a mother's body that make milk are called *mammary* glands. That is where the name *mammal* comes from.

Have you ever seen a mother cat before her kittens are born? She is fat because her kittens are growing inside her. The mammary glands on her belly are bigger than usual. They are getting ready to make milk. The nipples, or teats, at the ends of the glands stand out so the newborn kittens will be able to find them easily.

When the kittens are born, they are very small. Their eyes are closed tightly, they cannot hear, and they can hardly stand up. The mother cat licks each kitten clean as it leaves her body, and she may have to bite the cord that connects it to her. Then she lies down on her side, pushes her kittens toward her nipples, and continues to lick them. Somehow, by smell or touch, each blind, deaf, wobbly kitten finds a nipple and begins to suck. No one has to teach the kittens to suck; they do it naturally. Soon their little stomachs are full of milk and they go to sleep. The mother cat curls around them, keeping her babies warm and protected.

For a while the only food the kittens need is their mother's milk. They sleep and eat, eat and sleep, and every day they grow bigger and stronger on the milk their mother makes for them. After about three weeks, their eyes open, they can hear, and their legs give them support. Soon milk alone is not enough. The kittens start to eat solid food. They drink less and less milk, until finally their mother no longer makes it for them.

No one knows exactly when the first mammals appeared on earth. Fossils show us that the earliest mammals were alive about seventy million years ago, while dinosaurs walked the earth. These early mammals were small and shrewlike, and they remained that way until the dinosaurs died off. But in the millions of years that followed, the mammal populations grew and developed and changed.

Today we live in the age of mammals. There are thousands of different kinds of mammals on earth. The biggest animals, whales and elephants, are mammals. Tiny animals, mice and moles, are mammals. Flying animals, bats, are mammals. Jumping animals, kangaroos, are mammals. Dogs, cats, horses, and goats are mammals. Mammals live in the oceans, on land, in trees, in caves, and even in burrows deep in the ground. One kind of mammal, a human being, has even walked on the moon.

All these different kinds of mammals are alike in certain important ways. All mammals have a constant, warm body temperature. They all have some hair or fur. Their teeth are shaped so they can chew different kinds of food. Compared with other animals, mammal brains are large. All mammal babies develop inside their mothers' bodies. And all mammal mothers make milk in their mammary glands to feed their babies.

Mammary Glands and How Milk Is Made

Glands are found inside animals and even plants. They are made of groups of special cells whose job is to produce fluids that keep the plant or animal healthy and active. These fluids are called secretions. You have glands in your skin that make sweat when you are hot. Sweat is a secretion that cools you off. You have glands in your mouth that secrete saliva to keep your mouth moist and to help soften and digest the food you chew. Glands in your eyes secrete tears to keep your eyes free of dirt and dust. Glands deep inside your body make powerful secretions called hormones. Some hormones control your growth and development; others make you excited or let you sleep or even help you think.

Milk is the secretion made by the mammary glands of mammals. Mammary glands begin to form even before a mammal is born. They appear on either side of the body along the "milk lines" in the developing embryo. The milk lines disappear as the embryo grows, but the mammary glands remain.

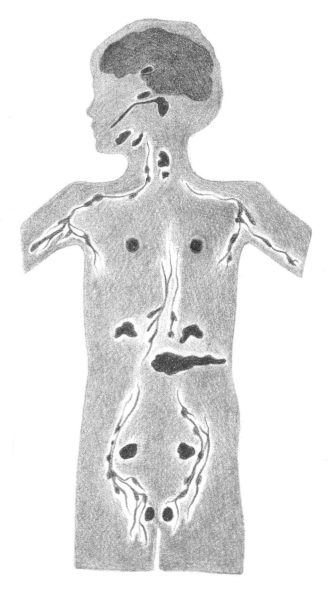

Most male and female mammals are born with mammary glands, but as they get older the glands develop differently. The male's do not grow. They remain small. The mammary glands of most female mammals stay small until the female becomes pregnant. Then the mammary glands begin to get larger. The mammary glands of human females enlarge when the female is old enough to become pregnant. Hormones are released that cause a pregnant female's body to change so that she can carry and nourish the embryo forming inside of her. Some of these hormones trigger the milk-making cells in her mammary glands. The milk-making cells make more cells and get ready to receive chemicals from other parts of her body. As soon as the baby is born, the cells go to work and the flow of milk begins.

There are millions of milk-making cells inside a mammary gland, and each one makes a tiny drop of whole milk. The cells are clustered together in clumps that look like bunches of grapes under the microscope. The milk droplets collect inside each "grape" in a hollow space called the lumen. Once a lumen is full, the milk passes through many small ducts, or tubes, that come together in a hard, round end—the nipple, or teat. It is just the right size to fit into the newborn mammal's mouth. When the newborn sucks on it, the milk comes out warm and sweet. We call this nursing, or suckling.

The first milk a mother makes is called colostrum. In humans it is thin and watery, just what a baby's digestive system needs in the first day or two of life. As the newborn continues to nurse, the milk-making cells make more and more milk.

Mammal mothers keep on making milk as long as their babies are nursing. In fact, the more a baby nurses, the more milk the mammary glands make. When the babies begin to eat solid food and nurse less often, the mammary glands make less milk. Mammal babies are said to be "weaned" when they no longer suck milk from their mothers. The milk-making cells gradually stop making milk, and the mammary glands shrink in size. They will not make milk again until the female has another baby.

How long do mammals give milk? It depends on the type of mammal. Lions nurse their cubs for about two months; dogs for six weeks; and humans for a year or more. Cows on dairy farms give milk for about ten months. Then they have to be mated and become pregnant again if they are to give more milk.

How Mammals Nurse Their Young

Nursing creates a strong bond between mammal mothers and their babies. Babies get food, warmth, and protection from their mothers. Mothers stay close to their babies after giving birth and seem to enjoy nursing and taking care of them.

The way mammal mothers and their young behave is not exactly the same for each mammal group. Some mammals stand and nurse their young in plain sight; others lie down in a hidden, protected spot. Some mammal babies nurse several times an hour; others nurse less frequently. Some mammal babies are well developed when they are born; others are not. The number of mammary glands a mammal mother has is related to the number of babies she can have.

Human mothers, apes, and the larger monkeys have two mammary glands, called breasts, on their chests. They usually have only one baby at a time and hold their infants in their arms while nursing. Many of these mothers carry their babies with them wherever they go.

A mother bear has four mammary glands and gives birth to her cubs in winter, while she is still hibernating in a cave or burrow. Usually only two cubs are born, but there can be as many as five. When a mammal mother gives birth to more than one baby at a time, we say she has a litter. The sleeping bear's litter of cubs nuzzle into her chest and nurse when they need to. When spring comes and the mother bear wakes up, she nurses her cubs from a sitting position.

Mother cats, lions, dogs, wolves, rats, and mice can all have litters. They have six pairs of mammary glands on their bellies, so they can feed many babies at once. These mothers usually lie on their sides while their babies nurse, often curling around them to keep them warm and protected. They lick their litters often and rarely leave to find food for themselves. Even after the babies' eyes are open and they begin to move about, the mothers stay close and nurse their litters many times a day.

A lioness usually has two or three cubs in an out-of-the way spot.

Puppies often shove and push as they find the nipples. Sometimes it is several minutes before the litter settles down.

Rats and mice can have as many as twelve babies in one litter and many litters a year. The babies' eyes and ears are closed when they are born, and they have no teeth or hair. The litter stays warm by huddling.

Newborn rabbits have no fur, but they do not get cold because their mother makes a warm nest for them. She lines it with fur from her chin and from her belly, which also makes it easy for her babies to find her teats. She can feed her litter quickly, because muscles in her mammary glands squirt milk into the babies' mouths. When their little bellies are full, the mother covers them with more fur and leaves the nest to find food for herself. At the end of the first week, the babies have fur of their own.

There are 900 different kinds of bats in the world, but most bat mothers give birth to only one rather large baby, called a pup. One kind of bat mother forms a pouch with her wings to catch her pup as it is born. Then she licks it clean. At first the newborn bat clings to one of its mother's nipples and feeds even while she is flying around. Later it hangs upside down from the ceiling of a cave, often among millions of other pups, while the mother goes out. Some scientists who study bats now believe that a returning mother can find her own pup by remembering its location, smell, and sound— but if she doesn't, she may end up nursing any pup that needs it.

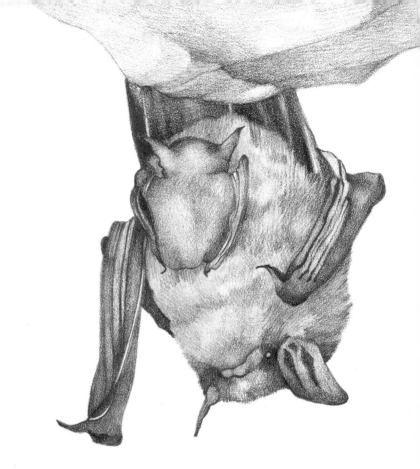

Guinea pig babies are born with well-developed teeth, so they can nibble solid food shortly after they are born. They do not need milk for more than a few days. This is lucky, since the mother normally has a litter of four babies but only has two teats.

Mother sheep, cows, goats, deer, horses, camels, rhinoceros, and giraffes all nurse their young standing up. They have two or four mammary glands enclosed in a sac, called an udder, that hangs down between their hind legs. The glands end in long teats, which stick our sideways when the udder is full of milk, making it easier for the babies to reach them.

These baby mammals can stand soon after birth. They duck under their mothers' bellies and nose around until they find the teats. Sometimes they butt and push with their heads to make more milk flow.

A foal three hours old can run so fast it is hard to catch.

An elephant mother usually has only one baby at a time, which she carries inside of her for almost two years and then nurses for about two years. The baby stands and nurses from two mammary glands between its mother's front legs. The baby's trunk is short and weak and is not used for drinking or picking up food right away.

A sow, a female pig, lies on her side, and the sucking of her piglets causes muscles in her mammary glands to squirt milk into their mouths. The piglets swallow as fast as they can.

A hippopotamus mother gives birth to one baby in shallow water and lies on her side while the baby nurses. The baby hippo can walk soon after it is born, and breathes at the surface of the water.

27

Mammals that live in the sea have two mammary glands close to their tails. A baby whale is born tail first into the water. Right away it must swim to the surface to breathe. Sometimes its mother and other female helpers, called "aunties," push the newborn up with their powerful heads. When the baby needs to nurse, it swims underwater and fastens on to one of its mother's nipples. Evidently it does not do much sucking, because muscles in the mother's mammary glands force out lots of milk very fast.

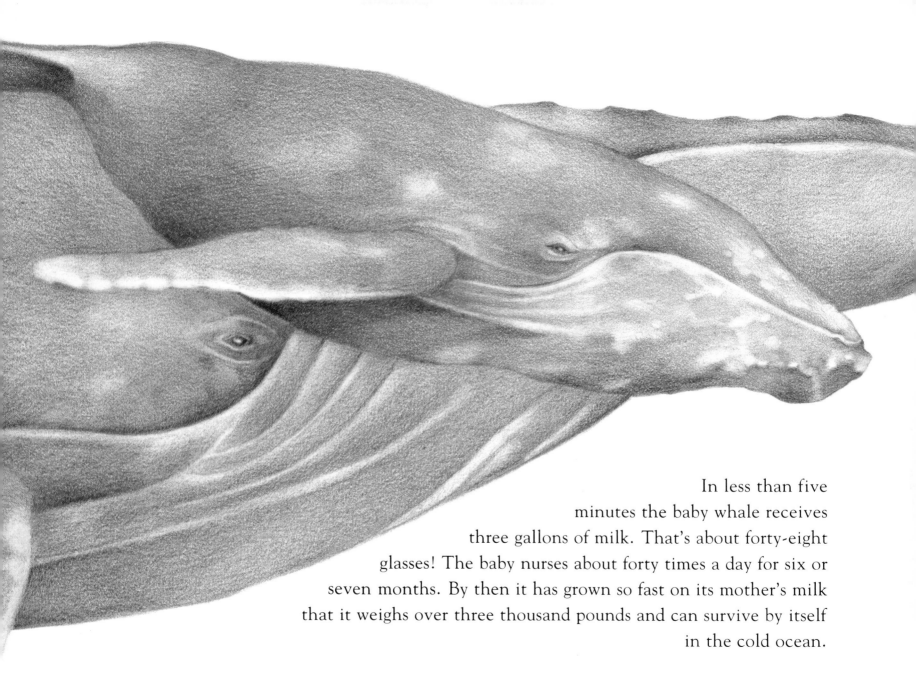

In less than five
minutes the baby whale receives
three gallons of milk. That's about forty-eight
glasses! The baby nurses about forty times a day for six or
seven months. By then it has grown so fast on its mother's milk
that it weighs over three thousand pounds and can survive by itself
in the cold ocean.

Mother kangaroos, opossums, and koala bears feed their young from mammary glands hidden inside a special pocket, or pouch, on their bellies. The young of these mammals are extremely small and helpless when they are born.

A newborn kangaroo, called a "joey," is only an inch long. Even so, right away it must crawl along its mother's belly to reach her pouch. Inside, it fastens on to one of her four nipples, almost swallowing it. For five months the joey does not let go. It grows very big on its mother's milk. In about eight months, it leaves to nibble solid food but still returns to the pouch to nurse. A mother kangaroo feeds her joey for about a year.

Opossum babies are so tiny that six can fit in a teaspoon. A mother opossum carries as many as thirteen nursing babies in her pouch at one time.

Two mammals are more primitive than all the others. They are the platypus and the spiny anteater. These mammal mothers have large eggs that start to develop into embryos in their bodies but then are coated with a shell and laid. The ducts from the mothers' mammary glands open directly onto their bellies and do not end in nipples. When the eggs hatch, the babies lap up the milk that oozes out.

What Milk Is Made From

Milk looks just about the same, no matter what mammal makes it. It is a white or slightly yellow liquid, and a little thick and sticky. That's why it leaves a film on the inside of a drinking glass. Fresh milk smells sweet, although milk may have a slight odor if the mother has eaten something peculiar. If a cow eats wild onions in the pasture, her milk will smell like onions.

Because milk is made from the food a mother eats and the chemicals stored in her body, a mother's health is very important. A nursing mother needs to eat more than usual. If her diet is poor, her milk will not contain all the nutrients her babies need.

All mammal milk has the same basic ingredients, although the amounts vary from one mammal group to another. The basic ingredients in milk are:

WATER

Milk is mostly water. Everything else is mixed in the water. Where does the water come from? From water that mothers drink and food they eat.

SUGAR

What makes milk sweet? Sugar does. Milk contains a special sugar, called lactose. You cannot see it, because it is dissolved in the water.

All lactose is exactly the same, no matter what mammal milk it comes from. To make lactose, the milk-making cells use two simpler sugars, glucose and galactose, that mammal mothers store in their bodies. Where do these sugars come from? From foods with sugar that mothers eat.

Lactose gives babies the energy they need to stay warm, to move, and to grow. It is easy for babies to digest. They have a special chemical, lactase, that breaks apart lactose. In fact, babies have more lactase than adults have, because they drink more milk.

Kangaroo milk has the most lactose, so it is the sweetest mammal milk. Seal milk has very little lactose, so it is not very sweet. Horse's milk is about as sweet as human milk. Cow's milk is less sweet.

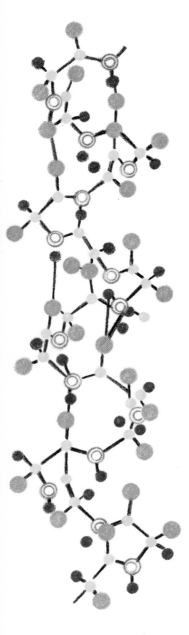

PROTEIN

Lactose makes milk sweet, but something else makes milk white and cloudy—protein. The main protein in milk is called casein. There are also other proteins in milk, called the whey proteins. Milk protein does not dissolve in water like lactose does. It stays in the water in very tiny particles that do not settle to the bottom. The particles are microscopic, so you cannot see them, but they make milk look "milky" white.

There are so many different proteins in nature that scientists do not know them all. Proteins are found in every cell of every plant and animal living on earth. Working together, they help make cells alive.

All the millions of different proteins have the same basic structure. They are all giant combinations of about twenty basic parts, called amino acids. Some people say that amino acids are "the building blocks of proteins." Amino acids are molecules that can hook together end to end to form long chains that twist and bend. The chains are the proteins. The number and order of the amino acids on the chain determine the protein that is formed.

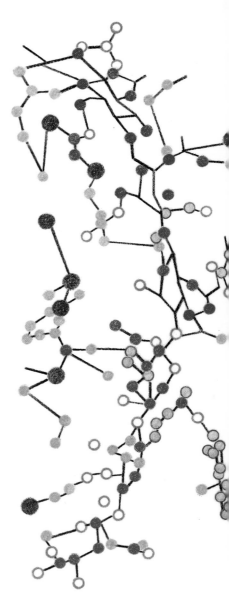

Only the milk-making cells in the mammary glands of mammals know how to put the amino acids together in the right order to make casein. Not all caseins are alike, however. Each type of mammal hooks the amino acids together in a slightly different order, so each mammal group makes a slightly different casein. The casein whales make is different from the casein cows make. And cow casein is different from bat casein, and so on.

A person who is "allergic" to milk is usually drinking milk from a non-human mammal. And it is usually the difference in casein that is causing the problem.

Where do the amino acids in milk protein come from? From foods with proteins that mothers eat, like meat, fish, eggs—and milk.

All mammal babies need casein. When a baby mammal digests its mother's milk, the amino acids in the casein unhook and travel to the growing parts of the baby's body. They help make muscles, blood, organs, nerves, brain cells, and other tissues. Cow's milk has slightly more protein than human milk, which is low in protein. Only apes and rhinoceros have as little protein in their milk as humans do.

The milk of some mammals, like hares and field mice, has lots
of protein, and their babies grow very fast.

FAT

The fat in milk is also called butterfat, because the butter you eat is made from this fat. Butterfat makes milk taste rich and gives it a yellowish color. Fat from different mammal's milk may smell and taste a little different.

Fat, like protein, does not dissolve in the water in milk. It exists in little droplets, or globules, that tend to stick together. Dairy companies homogenize milk to make the fat globules smaller and more evenly mixed in the milk. But if you find milk that has not been homogenized and let it stand for a while, you can see the butterfat. It will rise to the top and float. This top layer is called cream, and it is used to make ice cream, whipping cream, and butter. Skim the cream off, and you have skimmed milk.

The fat in milk helps newborn babies store extra food and energy in their bodies. It also coats developing nerves. Baby mammals born in cold parts of the world, like caribou and reindeer, and those that live in the sea, like whales and seals, need lots of fat right away as insulation to keep them warm.

Baby whales and seals quickly gain a layer of fat, called blubber, that keeps them from losing body heat into the water and helps make them buoyant. Milk from these cold-climate mammals has so much butterfat that it is almost like heavy cream. Milk from cows and goats has about as much butterfat as human milk. Milk from donkeys and horses has very little butterfat.

Where does the fat in milk come from? Mothers can make it in their bodies from many foods they eat, including foods with fats and oils in them, like nuts, plant oils, and fatty meat.

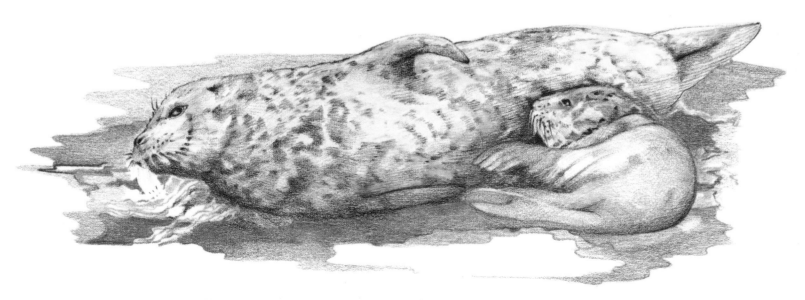

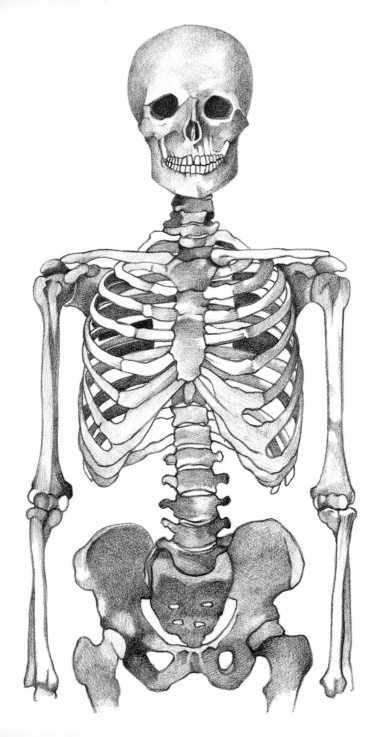

MINERALS

Two important minerals are dissolved in the water of milk—calcium and phosphorus. Young mammals need both to form hard, strong bones and teeth. Cow's milk has more calcium and phosphorus than human milk. Traces of other minerals—zinc, iron, and magnesium—are also found in milk, and these help babies grow. Where do the minerals in milk come from? From foods rich in minerals, like dark green vegetables, that mothers eat.

VITAMINS

Milk contains many vitamins. Vitamin A, which makes sharp eyes, and vitamin D, which builds strong bones, are both dissolved in the fat. So are vitamins K and E. The B vitamins, which help make blood and aid in growth, are dissolved in the water. So is vitamin C, which helps prevent some diseases. Where do the vitamins in milk come from? From all the foods that mothers eat.

ANTIBODIES

Antibodies are special proteins that animals make to help fight off diseases in their environment. Horses, cows, sheep, and pigs are born without antibodies. They have to get them from the antibodies in their mother's colostrum in order to survive. Soon they make their own. Human babies are born with antibodies they received from their mothers while they were still developing inside them. Nevertheless, their mothers' milk contains an antibody that helps keep the babies from getting diarrhea. Soon they make all their own, too.

The milk-making cells in mammary glands put all these ingredients together in a way that is just right for mammal babies. Milk from each mammal group is a truly perfect food for the babies in that group. Cow's milk is the perfect milk for calves. Mare's milk is perfect for foals. Dolphin's milk is the perfect food for dolphin pups. And so on.

Dairy Animals Around The World

Mammal mothers make milk for their babies, but milk from one kind of mammal can sometimes be drunk by another kind of mammal. Thousands of years ago, human beings learned to keep other mammals and use their milk and the food that can be made from it. Pictures on Egyptian tombs show oxen-like animals being milked. Ancient people in Asia milked sheep and goats. Keeping cows for milk probably started in Europe.

Mammals that are kept for their milk are called dairy animals. The American Indians never kept mammals for milk. Dairy cows were first brought to North America, to Jamestown, in 1607. Today there are different breeds of cows in the United States, but the most common is the Holstein, because it gives the most milk.

People around the world keep dairy animals that live naturally in their region. In many places, the milk is used more to make butter and cheese than to drink, because these foods last longer. Adults from races or cultures that never kept dairy animals may have a hard time digesting the lactose in milk. These people drink very little milk or else use dairy products free of lactose.

If you lived in the mountains of Nepal, you might drink yak milk. In India, water buffalo are a source of milk. If you lived in the deserts of Saudi Arabia, you might drink camel milk. In some parts of Asia, people drink mare's milk. In the Andes Mountains of South America, people keep llama herds for their milk. Goats and sheep are popular milk-producing animals in France, Greece, Italy, and Spain. Reindeer milk is used by people living in the cold areas of Norway and Finland.

Mammals feed their own babies and share their milk the world over.

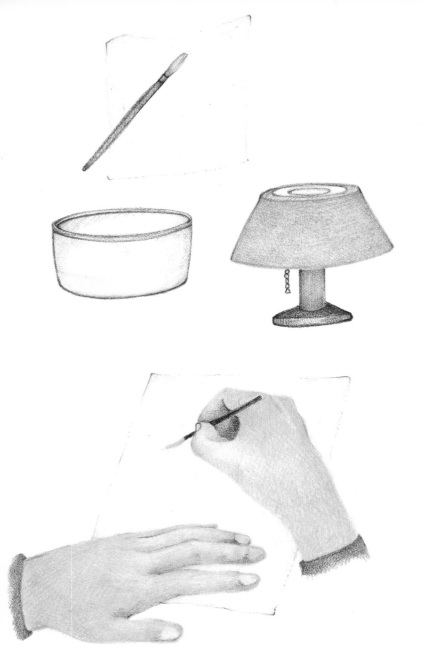

Fun You Can Have With Milk
Secret Writing

What you need: a thin brush or a toothpick; a little milk in a dish; plain white paper; a lamp

What to do:

1. Dip the brush or toothpick into the milk and write a secret message on the paper. Use enough milk to soak into the paper, but not so much that it runs or smears.

2. When you are finished, let the milk dry completely. Nothing will show on the paper.

3. To see the message, hold the paper over a light bulb that is on, close enough that the paper warms up but not so close that it burns. The message will begin to appear as soon as the paper gets hot.

The message becomes visible because the heat turns the sugar (lactose) and protein (casein) brown.

Making Yogurt

What you need: one pint of milk; a pot and stirring spoon; a plastic container or glass jar with lid; a carton of store-bought plain yogurt; a stove, and someone to help you with it.

What to do:

1. Heat the milk until it is warm but not boiling. Let it cool slightly.

2. Add two tablespoons of the plain yogurt to the milk and stir. Pour into the container and cover.

3. Leave the container in a warm spot in the kitchen overnight. The oven is a good place if there is a pilot on; or else have someone warm the oven slightly. Put the mixture in, *make sure the oven is off*, and keep the door closed.

4. The next day, take a look at what you have. Taste it.

Yogurt contains two kinds of bacteria. The bacteria in the yogurt you added to the milk used the milk as food and changed the milk sugar (lactose) into acid (lactic acid). This extra acid caused all the small particles of the protein casein to clump together and form what we call curds. Stir it all up and you have—yogurt! Save some of this to start another batch.

Watching Changes in Milk

What you need: a cup of milk; a clear glass bottle or drinking glass; foil

What to do:

1. Pour a cup of milk in the bottle or glass and cover the top lightly with foil.
2. Watch the bottle for a week or longer to see what happens. Do not shake the bottle! Otherwise you won't be able to see the changes.

What to look for:

1. In the first few days there is not much to see. But if you smell the milk you can tell something is happening. Keep it covered and keep watching.
2. In a few more days you will see the milk start to separate into two layers. There is a thick, lumpy,

white layer at the bottom, the curd. On the top is a thin, watery, slightly cloudy layer, called the whey. Curd is pressed and flavored to make cheese. Whey can be dried and used for animal food.

3. Keep the milk bottle longer, and you will see even more changes. After a couple of weeks the curd will disappear and only a foul-smelling greyish liquid will be left. *Here is why:* Milk contains bacteria and other invisible microbes that come from the air, the environment, and the body of the mammal that made it. The bacteria use the milk as food and change the sugar into acid (lactose into lactic acid). The acid causes the protein casein to lump together on the bottom. This is the curd. The other proteins form the whey. In time, the microbes completely spoil the milk, and it is not good for anything. The more microbes in the milk, the faster this happens. Dairy companies heat milk by a process called pasteurization to kill some of the microbes in milk. We keep milk in the refrigerator because most microbes do not grow so quickly in the cold, and the milk lasts longer.

Index